Network Marketing

The Fastest Way to Become a Rockstar of Network Marketing and Build Your Team, Serve Others and Make Your Dream Come True

By:

Rick Loftus

Published by 42 Enterprises Publishing,

All Rights Reserved,
Copyright 2016, Cincinnati, Ohio

Table of Contents

Introduction 3

Chapter 1: Network Marketing Basics....................................... 4

Chapter 2: Attaining Success in Network Marketing 10

Chapter 3: Building Your Team through Network Marketing 14

Chapter 4: Serving Others 17

Chapter 5: Network Marketing Tips, Tricks and Strategies that Work 20

Chapter 6: Network Marketing Mistakes to Avoid 25

Conclusion 29

Introduction

Network marketing is not a new type of business in the country. So many people have joined network marketing programs and they are doing very well especially those who joined the most popular businesses. It is a business venturethat attracts people who want tostart a business but they do not have alarge sum of money as capital, likemanybusinessesdemand. Network marketing is also a good business venture for people who have little time in a day because it is not as involving as other businesstypes. You can do this kind of business during your part time and make so much money.

Other than making money, network marketing connects you to so many people, and gives you a chance to meet new and influential people who can teach you a lot of things in life. If done well, this is a type of business that can place you in a great position not just financially but socially.

Many people have joined network marketing programs blindly and they lost so much money because they did not have enough information about running such businesses. That is why this is a great eBook to read. It has all the things you need to learn in order to start such a business well to attain success in the future. You need to know the kinds of skills you need to get started for instance, how to join a network marketing program, how to start networking and how to make more money, all of which have been covered here.

Chapter 1: Network Marketing Basics

Network marketing refers to a business model in which a network of distributors is needed in order to build the business. In such kind of businesses, payouts are made at more than one level, depending on how many levels the business has already grown. This is a type of business that is gaining so much popularity today as people look for a part-time job opportunities where they can make more money to supplement their full time salaries. It is also a good business venture for someone that is looking for a flexible kind of business which can be operated with ease, unlike other types of businesses.

Onething that attracts many people tothese kindsof business is because of their low initialinvestment. The money is used to purchase a sample kit ofthe products that the company is dealing with,then you are required to sell theproduct line to a friend, a colleague or a family friend. Once you sell to people close to you, they will do the same to people in their contacts list, and the network will eventually be formed.

Some programs will require you to recruit some sales representatives, and when you get a few sales representatives, their sales will also generate some income for you, who is above them in the program.

There is no way a network marketing program will survive on recruitments only, other than selling its products. This is in fact an easy way to tell if the program is genuine or not. A program has to generate some money, which will be used to compensate its participants, therefore if the program you are participating in does not have products to sell, it could be illegal.

Unfortunately, network marketing programs are not under any kind of regulation by the government bodies or non-government bodies. You therefore have to do your own due diligence before you join any network to ensure that you are not losing your money in the end. A lot of people have invested in illegal network marketing programs in the past, which is why it is good to conduct a thorough investigation before you invest your money into any such program.

Reasons to join network marketing programs

Withall that said, would you like to join a network marketing program? You probably have receivedpropositionsfrom your friend, family or colleagues tojoin their program. The thing is that different network marketingprogramsdiffer so much but one thing that is commonin allof them is the promise that you might haveto do away with your full timeemployment because of the benefits that you get through networking.

One ofthethings that attracts many people to network marketing is the fact that youend up being your own boss, and there is always a great chance of making a lot of money if you are able to recruit more people to the program. Above all, you get to meet morepeople, who can impact your life in so many ways. There are always great benefits to consider as these are the onesthat will attract you to invest in this kind of business.

Network marketing is particularly good for retirees who have some money and less energy to work in order to multiply their retirement savings. Ifyou are getting close to retirement, it is good to think clearly about retirement and how you are going to survive when your income stops coming in. Even with retirement money, you are not guaranteed that you will be absolutely safe for the many years that you willlive after retirement. It is therefore important tothink of a way to save your money or to invest what you have in order to earn a little more that could go a long way to help you cater for your needs a little longer after retirement. For a lot of retirees, network marketing comes as a great alternative because there is a chance that you will be getting some money every now and then, which can supplement the retirement savings you have already received.

Another good reason to get started into network marketing is the chance that the program can grow so much in a short period of time. Imagine the many people who are already jobless and others are in jobs that are frustrating them. These people are definitely looking for something easer yet big and one that can promise them something great in the end. All these people are likely to join network marketing for the same benefits you are eying.

You will lovenetworkmarketing because of its direct selling programs, which are much better than any other business that an entrepreneurship cantake. With network marketing, you benefit fromtraining, support, from encouragement and motivation, which goes a long way to keep you in business for long time. Even when things are tough, you do not give up and this is what brings good results in the end. Retirees for instance get a chance to stay busy, relevant, connected to other people, in great health, and they get a better way to spend their energy and time. The companies offer other benefits to participants in order to give them a better reason to get in and make some money.

How to join

Networking companies manufacture different types of products that are very beneficial and rare in the market, then they pay people to be their sales people. These sales people are also rewarded for recruiting other people under their network to be sales people for the company. It is usually a commission kind of pay, where you are paid as per the amount of money you make from the sale.

Joining a network marketing program is very easy. Here are great steps that will get you in:

- ➢ Pick a good program to join, one that matches your interest. You have to identify what you are looking for in a network marketing program in order to pick a company that will offer just that. With so many network marketing companies operating in the country today, you have to be sure that you are choosing a good one. Again, you can chose a company that is dealing with products that you are interested in.

- ➢ Look for mentors. Mentors are very crucial in this kind of business. They willencourage you, help you and support you all the way to ensure that you are remaining firm in the business for you to enjoy thebenefitsthat comes with it. The person who will recruit you to the program will obviously be your mentor but you need other mentors, who will be close to you to help you network with as many people as you can.

- ➢ Start with a plan. You will need a good plan on how you will make your sales and how you will get people under you to ensure that you are making a good income ever week or month. You need to set a target on your plan so as to ensure that by the end of the stated period of time, you will have attained the goals you have set to achieve. State the strategies that you will use in order to achieve your goals. If for instance you want to recruit about 5 people by the end of themonth, you have to state clearly how you will go about it. This makes execution of the plan easy.

➢ Get down to business. You need to identify good people who will be able to work hard to network, just like you in order to keep the chain longer. This is what will be earning you some money every week. Once you get a few people to join the program under you, motivate them and ensure that you work with them to keep the network going on.

Skills network marketers need

There are habits and skills that network marketers need to develop and master in order to succeed in network marketing and these are for instance:

1) Connecting with people. Network marketing is all about creating connections with people as these are the ones who will join your network for you to earn something from the business. Creating connections with people does not have to be hard; you just need to learn how to speak in an influential manner to your family, friends or colleagues. Use any means possible to make them understand what you are dealing with and give them the benefits of joining your network.

2) Being able to share the opportunity. You should be able to sell the opportunity to as many people as possible therefore whenever there is a chance, you should be able to approach them and sell the idea to them. Always bring all the materials you will need for a proper presentation in the least time possible. If done well, such presentations can earn you so many clients in the long run.

3) Making a follow up. Not everyone will buy your idea immediately after a presentation; there are people who will need time to think about it. You need to know how to make a proper follow up without looking desperate. When talking to a potential customer, you should gauge them to know if they are really interested in such an opportunity. These are the people you should follow up on in order to see if they are still interested in the idea. With follow-ups, you have to practice the skill as much as it is necessary until it is fully mastered.

4) Training. You will be training people much of the time, especially the people who will join your network, therefore you need great skills to be able to effectively train and coach them on how they will be selling and recruiting their friends and family to the network. You will be the one teaching your customers on how they will overcome the obstacles to attain success in the business.

Chapter 2:
Attaining Success in Network Marketing

Network marketing may be the right business for you especially if you are looking for a way through which you can supplement your income and you only have a little amount of money as capital. You will not be required to present any qualifications in order to join a network marketing program and you will not be required to wait for a long time in order to start making money.

Many people have joined network marketingprograms and they startedmaking money after a week or two. This is determined by a fewfactorsthough, the main one being how fast you are able to sell your products or to bring in more people into the program.

Succeeding in network marketing is not always a guarantee. A few factors come into play toensure that you are making a good income out of networking and proceeds from the program's products. Here are some of thefactorsthat will lead to success in network marketing:

Choosing the right network marketing company to join

This is always a challenge for many people who have great interest in network marketing. Today, there are so many network marketing companies in the country and out of the country and all of them are offering great benefits to the people who will join them. It is important to know that not all of them are as good as they say, therefore be careful even as you use the opportunities they are offering to choose a good program join. Some programs are just there to waste your time and to steal your hard earned money.

The reason why many people are lured into illegal programs is because people are always excited whenever they see an opportunity to make money and they jump into the opportunity without taking time to think about it. It is important for people to only go for the idea when they are absolutely sure that it is the right one.

How do you choose the right network to join?

    a) By considering the types of products offered

        Network marketing is mainly involved with selling, and you will be doing the sales once you join the program. How fast you sell and the number of people you will sell to will always be determined by the types of products that you will be selling to them. You have to choose products that you are sure people will be interested in, so as to sell more to them, which is the only way you will be making some profits from it all.

        People buy products that can be consumed more than the other types of products. You have to ensure that the products you are selling are unique and scarce, with great benefits to the buyers for them to show an interest in them. The last thing you need is to sell something that consumers can easily find in the market. Ensure that you are choosing products with minimal competition.

        Choose products that are simple and easy to use too. Ensure that the products are meeting the needs of the people, just as the manufacturer promised.

b) By considering the commissions offered

The commission structure represents how the company will be paying you for the sales and the recruitments. This is a great factor in determining a good program to join. Some programs do not have a clear way through which they reward their members. You need to be careful not to be trapped by such programs. The right networking system should show how its members will be rewarded for every product that you will sell and every person that you will bring into the program. Some programs will give a sum that is too good to be true; you have to be careful about these ones as well.

c) By considering what the main emphasis is

Network marketing programs are all about recruitment and sales. People are rewarded for both selling and also recruiting new people to the program. Like I mentioned above, sales are the ones that will generate the income, which will be used to pay you. A program that emphasizes only on recruits may not be the best one to go for, and it could be a scam. Such programs are only interested in the money that the members are bringing in and they have no plans to pay them.

d) The length of time the business has been in operation

New network marketing companies are always not the best to run to whenever you are looking for a good place to invest your money. Some will use the best commissions to attract investors only to frustrate them a few months down the line. It is good to invest your money in a network marketing company that has been in business for a long time. Go for many years as this means that the business is already well established and there is a guarantee that you will not lose you money.

e) The company's reputation

It is always good to know what people are saying about a network marketing company that you are about to invest in. People are not always wrong and they might point out things that you did not know about the company, which can determine if the company is a good one to invest in or not. For you to know what people have to say about it, conduct a smart research and look for testimonials and feedback from people who have invested in the company. The internet will help you so much in finding the right information about a company of your interest. From what you will get, you should be able to evaluate whether the company is actually good to invest in or not.

Chapter 3:
Building Your Team through Network Marketing

Network marketing is more about recruiting, just as it is about selling. This does not mean that you will be waiting for potential clients outside their offices or in supermarkets, spotting the best dressed and sending endless emails and links to the people you think would be interested in your idea. This is a wrong approach to do this. You have to be smart if you want to gain the right types of customers. You also have to be patient if you want to build a strong network that will keep you in business for a long time.

Just like everyone else, you are chasing money, and just like everyone else is doing it smart, you also have to be smart and tactical. One of the things that network marketers need to avoid is becoming desperate. There is always the best way to do this, and this is the way everyone should be looking for in order to approach the right customers who will give you a sale and also join your network.

There are different methods and approaches that one can use in order to gain customers, and begging for them to join your network is not in the list. Here are a few proven tactics that will help you build a strong team in the shortest time possible:

i) Start Blogging

You can start your own blog about network marketing and see how people respond to it. Blogging is the best way for people to send messages these days, and so many people from all walks of life are reading blogs today. This could be the right way to start telling people what you already know and hear what they have to say about network marketing. People who will benefit from your information will contact you for more details and they could join you and start doing business with you.

You however have to learn how to capture people's attention for them to start reading your blog. You will have to use all the tools available and strategies that you can find in order to create the best blog about network marketing that everyone will want to read before they make the final decision to start such a business.

ii) *Use heightened blogging*

People who are smart use optimized blogging these days in order to get what they need from customers. This is the kind of blogging that will intrigue a potential buyer and also increase your chances of getting a high rank in Google or any other search engine. Take time if you want to blog about your great idea and give people justwhat they need to hear in orderto make the best decision that also suits your interests. Chooseuniquestrategiesthatno one else has used in the past and use graphics and videos too. Encourage discussion andsee how many people will show interest in what you are selling.

Take time to elaborate every point you put across and provide clear instructions to everything that your potential clients need to know. Leave room forthem to ask questions and clarifications and get back to them on time. You will have so many people interested in your idea in just a few days andyour blog willhit the internet to reach out to so many people in a short period of time.

iii) Dedication and commitment

You will have to dedicate enough time and effort to your team in order to strengthen it. Show your customers some love and concern and help them where possible. A good networking team has to work together in order to get a good foundation, which will be used to pull the team together even when times are tough. Every member of the team needs to know their commitment to the team and how much their efforts mean to the entire team. This way, they can work harder knowing that they have a part to play for the success of the business.

It is important to know that the commitment of every individual is the one that brings success to the entire team. You therefore have to lead by example and through your commitment, the other members can learn how much commitment benefits the business.

Chapter 4:
Serving Others

Network marketing is all about customers because the most important thing is to sell the company's products. People choose to sell such products this way because it is the only best way to sell important products as you create awareness about the existence of some of the most important products that are known to only a few people.

Network marketing is all about recommending and selling the products that you use to your friends, colleagues and family. These are the people that will form a network with you, and connect your network to the already existing network in the company.

Since this is all about better service to your customers, here are things you need to bear in mind:

- ✓ You are providing services to customers, because you are in the business of helping people with the products that you are selling. Once you join the network, you will have great responsibility to your customers; that is to help them live a healthier life and also to help them attain financial freedom. This is a business like any other, so you have to work hard to ensure that many people are benefitting from what you are selling in the end.

    You therefore have to focus on the products that you are selling, knowing that you are competing with other network marketing companies out there. You have the obligation of helping your company to compete successfully against other network marketing companies.

It is also important to know that this will be very easy for you, because it is always easy to sell a product than to sell a dream.

- ✓ Ensure that the product you are selling is the right one for the people you are selling it to. Do not use deceiving words to sell a product to a customer because this eventually backfires on you. You have to think of ways through which your product is beneficial to the people you are selling it to. Are they going to enjoy a huge saving for their money when they buy from you other than another company? Is the product more effective than what they have been using in the past? Is it a product that is offering a solution they have always looked for? These are some of the things you can consider in order to sell effectively to your customers.

Ensure that you give your customers all the information they need in order for them to make an informed decision. Allow them some time to explore the options they have, so that they can get back to you later on. This is how you build trust with your customers and show them that you only have their best interest at heart.

- ✓ Are the people you are targeting interested in the business opportunity you are offering? At times you will rush to sell the idea to a customer that is not interested in it and they will not even give you time to finish talking about it. Youcan easily get frustrated if you have not prepared yourself well. There is always a good way to approach someone that can becomeagood customer. You can for instance start by explaining the benefits they can get from the products you are selling, then show them the cheapest way to get the product. You can for instance show them how important such a product is to many people and how they can sell to their friends too. Some of your customers will only be contented about buying the product and not joining the network. This should be okay with you. The only mistake you can make is in coercing people tojoin the network, which is not possible especially if you have not given them any time to do their own research for effective decision making.

You have to be good to your customers and teach them what they need to know about the product and a chance to do business with you. This way, they will do what is right to the customers they will get and you will have a solid network thereafter. This is what will keep all of you in business for long time.

Chapter 5:
Network Marketing Tips, Tricks and Strategies that Work

Every business is bound to succeed if the business owner will take time to master a few tricks, tips and strategies that will get him the results he is looking for. Networking marketing business is no exceptional. There are the obvious tips that will get you clients in any kind of business for instance taking action without delay, being a leader in your own business or building a list of clients that you can always rely on. However, there are other strategies, tips and tricks that are unique to every business type and these are the ones you should be looking for in order to succeed in internet marketing. Here are a few tricks, tips and strategies that should get you started in network marketing:

Arm yourself with knowledge-

Network marketing is a tricky affair, therefore it can posea greatchallenge for anyone that is not familiar with the real business. For you to get started on the right footing and to succeed in thiskind of business, you need to ensure that you have great knowledge up your sleeves. There are MLM scams all over the internet today and so many people have fallen into such traps without knowing it. Knowledge will keep you away from such scams and ensure that you are conducting your business safely and successfully. Remember that the more you know about the business the better you will be able to protect yourself from fraudsters and scammers and the better you can come up with a plan for success.

Use of PR to create awareness-

Word of mouth remains the most effective marketing strategy that will get your products out there to consumers who could be interested in them. How else will they know what you are offering and how it will benefit them? A few year ago, marketers used word-of-mouth to build their network marketing programs but these days,with the advancement in computertechnology, it is very easy toget the word out there to a lot of prospective customers. You can do this in so many ways, for instance by use of blogging sites. You can use bloggers to reviewyour products and company, with agreatcall-for–action which willgetthe readers inquiring more aboutthe companyandtheproducts.

Always mention the people who influence your business-

These should be popular business people who are already successful in the business. What you want with this is to build credibility and to show your prospective customers your expertise. It is good for business if you associate yourself with successful people, who have a good reputation in the market, people will associate you with the successful business person and would be quick to show their interest in your business, because they can now trust you. Many successful business people have a great follow up who are waiting for a chance to connect to the big name. This is the chance you will be providing to people once you associate your business to a certain influencer of their interest.

Use of social media-

There are social sites that are specifically used by network marketers. These are the ones you should join in order to learn more about network marketing and also connect to people with the same line of business with you. IBO Toolbox is a popular social site that is used by network marketers from all over the world. In the site, you will learn so much, including different ways through which you can promote your business and strategies that you can use in order to grow your network. You can also make your network marketing program popular through use of such platforms. This is what will get people to your network for a successful business in the long run.

Learn how to attract the right customers-

So much time can be wasted if you will start selling your idea to all people you meet along the way, even those who have no interest in network marketing. It will be much easier if you know the right people, with interest in network marketing and money to invest in such kind of business. Consumers search for all types of information online these days, and this is the platform you should use in order to connect to people who are interested in what you are offering. Choose the right keywords to look for people online for instance keywords like join, buy, distributor, purchase, order, discount and such like keywords that are used in network marketing.

Choose a company with products that you love-

Any business is bound to succeed if the business person is passionate about it and this is mainly determined by the love a

business person has for the products or services that he is offering. There is no way you will succeed in a business that you have no liking for, that is why you need to choose the type of business to invest in wisely. You need to be proud of what you are selling as this is the only way you will get to explain it to your customers and convince them about buying it. Network marketing is also not something that you do for a few months and then get out of it. Imagine doing business for a long time yet you do not like it at all? You should therefore be sure that you are excited about the products that you are selling in order to stay in that business for a long time, working hard to get people into the network and selling more every day.

Provide testimonials-

Trust is a very important element in any business. People will want to do business with a brand or someone that they trust. Byproviding testimonials, prospective clients will understand the kind of a business person you are better and this can make them trust you even more. Testimonials expose you to people who are looking for business people like you. Through testimonials, so many people can showinterest to what you are dealing with. Share your results and your success too and so many people will identify with you.

Use of TV adverts-

So many people watch TV in the country and there are specific times when people watch more TV than other times.Advertisers place their ads during such times when they know that a lot of people are watchingtheirTV. This should bethe time you are placing your advert too, in order to capturethe attention of prospective networkmarketers who could be interested in what you aredealing with. Intercept advertising traffic and place your advert where you are sure that so many people will get to see it.Good thing is that these days, so many people are showing interest in network marketing as they look for a cheaper way to start a business that can generate an income to supplement what they already have. That is why they might be interested in your ad.

Chapter 6:
Network Marketing Mistakes to Avoid

Just like every other business, network marketing is full of ups and downs and many people make mistakes that deny them the chance to enjoy the full benefits that the business has to offer. There are so many people that are striving to make money online these days and since there is no sufficient information online, they end up making mistakes that they could regret thereafter.

In order to make money in network marketing, you have to follow the right guidelines and use the right strategies to acquire the right customers. You also have to avoid making mistakes that can eat up your profits and your capital, leaving you with minimum or no benefits in the end. Here are some of the common mistakes network marketers all over the world make and how you can avoid them:

   a. Following other people blindly

   This happens all the time, where people follow other people without really knowing what they are getting themselves into. Many people get into business because peoplethey know are already in those businesses and they realize their mistakes later on, when they have already lost so much time and money. Youhave to take time to study the kind of network marketing your friends, family orcolleagues are into and how they are making money before you jump in.

   Do not copy what other people are doing either, hoping that it will work out from you the same way it has worked for them. You have to dedicate sometime into studying what you need to know then work hard to make your own business thrive.

b. Making your business sound too good to be true

When trying to attract customers, a lot of people feel that exaggerating a little bit will get them the number of customers they are looking for. Many people believe that giving people exactly what they are looking for is a sure way to attract them to buy your product or to join your network. In order to enjoy lasting results, you have to stick to facts when it comes to network marketing. Understand that network marketing is not meant for all people and that not everyone will be interested in the products that you are selling. That is why you should be realistic whenever you are selling your ideas to the people so as to only attract people who will be happy with your business idea and products.

c. Getting too attached to the company or the product that you are selling.

Many people do not see a problem in this until they realize that they cannot think of other ways to make money through network marketing. Focusing so much on the company or the product makes it hard for you to see other ways and opportunities to make money through network marketing. You will remain in the same position for a long time instead of growing and attaining your success in the business.

What you should do is tell your customers what the product is all about and be quick to move to another product that may work better than the previous one, instead of holding so much on the product that may not be selling as much as you should be selling.

d. Lack of commitment or focus

Network marketing is a business that will require so much of your attention for it to grow to what you want it to become. Commitment andyour focus on the business is whatwill give you the kinds of results that youare eying. First of all, do not jump from one thing to the other once you sign up for network marketing, this is the only thing you should be doing for it to succeed. You need totake time to understand the operations of the companyyou have invested money in for instance and time to get the right customers for the products that you are selling. This is only possible if you have time to run the business.

e. Not Conducting a thorough research

Before signing up for network marketing with a company, you need to be sure that it is the right company you want to work with. Some companies provide great information and hide so much, which is hard toknow if youwill not take time to research well about it. Some negative feedback from previous clients for instance may not be put in the front pages of the company's profile because the company knows so well that this could drive prospective customers away. Toget such information, you have to dig deeper into thehistory and past operations of the business. This will take time but in the end, you will know the kind of company you are about to invest your money into.

f. Trying to start in your own company

   Network marketing is a tricky affair. You need to acquire the networking skills as well as the experience to be able to reinvent your own wheel. If you are new to network marketing, you are better off starting in the network marketing programs that have already been started. Starting your own program when you are new in business may backfire on you and this means losing so much money and so much lost time. Take time to study the things that work and those that do not work. You can in the end plan to improve on what is already there instead of trying to create something that already has been created by so many people.

g. Neglecting upline support

   One of the things you will need somuch inthiskind of business is support. Networkmarketers thrive in the support they get frompeople who are up in thenetwork. Sometimesyou might think that you do not really need their support, and think that you might be bothering them if you ask for help and support. This is a great mistake becausetheir support is what will help you get a good network under you, whichwillkeep youenjoying thebenefits form thebusiness. What network marketers should knowis that the upline support is what will give you success in business. If therefore you are planning to fail in this business, neglect the support and help that they offer to you. Do not think that you are too experienced to require anyone's help. Accept the help and support and build a network that will give you so many sales thereafter.

Conclusion

Network marketing is slowly gaining popularity as a great alternative for people who are looking for a good place to invest a little amount of money for great financial benefits and other great benefits like a chance to meet and connect with great people who can impact your life in so many ways. Network marketing programs that have already been established are many and other programs are coming up so fast in order to meet the unending demand for people who want to experience network marketing and to grow their business in a business that does not require much.

Succeeding in network marketing does not come automatically though. There are things you have to do, for instance working hard to sell and to attract great people to join the network. You also have to be ethical and genuine in business in order to attract people who will stay in business for a long as it is necessary. There are network companies that have been in existence for so many years already and they have survived the odds in the market because they sell genuine products that are scarce in the market, which are offering great benefits to consumers. These are the types of companies to join if you want to succeed in MLM.

Be prepared and acquire as much information as you can about network marketing and the company you are about to join as this is the only way you will be able to deal with all the hurdles that you will meet along the way.